D0824674

FRIENDSHIP BRACELETS AND BEADING FUN

25 knotty, dotty, stripey and sparkly designs to make!

Petra Boase

ARMADILLO

This edition is published by Armadillo, an imprint of Anness Publishing Ltd, Blaby Road, Wigston, Leicestershire LE18 4SE; info@anness.com

www.annesspublishing.com

If you like the images in this book and would like to investigate using them for publishing, promotions or advertising, please visit our website www.practicalpictures.com for more information.

Publisher: Joanna Lorenz
Senior Editor: Sue Grabham
Project Editors: Lyn Coutts, Charlotte Evans, Richard McGinlay
Photographer: John Freeman
Production Controller: Mai-Ling Collyer

PUBLISHER'S NOTE
Although the advice and information in this book are believed to be accurate and true at the time of going to press, neither the authors nor the publisher can accept any legal responsibility or liability for any errors or omissions that may have been made nor for any inaccuracies nor for any loss, harm or injury that comes about from following instructions or advice in this book.

Manufacturer: Anness Publishing Ltd, Blaby Road, Wigston, Leicestershire LE18 4SE, England
For Product Tracking go to: www.annesspublishing.com/tracking
Batch: 0610-22728-1127

Introduction

Friendship bracelets are a symbol of companionship, which is why they make such fun presents for your friends and family. They do not need much equipment and they are not expensive or difficult to make. In fact, you can make a bracelet almost anywhere! Make them to match your best outfits, or try experimenting with different shades of material. If you are braiding a bracelet for a friend, why not use the shades they like best? You could also make identical bracelets for you and all your best friends to wear.

But the fun does not stop there. You will learn how to decorate your creations with dangling beads and how to weave beads into bracelets and necklaces. These look very professional and will impress your friends no end.

Once you have the knack of braiding and beading, let your imagination run wild and design your very own range of accessories.

Petra Boase

Contents

Materials

BADGE PIN
A badge pin is glued on to the back of a badge so that it can be fastened to an item of clothing.

BEADS
Beads come in a wide variety of different sizes, shades, textures and patterns. Tiny or small beads usually have very small holes, so it is easier to thread them on to fine sewing thread, or to sew them on to items using needle and thread. Medium and large size beads are perfect for using with thicker yarns.

BRACELET/NECKLACE CLAMP
This can be fastened over the knot at each end of a friendship cord to finish it off. Bracelet or necklace fasteners can be attached to clamps.

BRACELET/NECKLACE FASTENER
This is a releasable metal clasp that can be used to secure a friendship bracelet or necklace.

BRACELET/NECKLACE THREAD
This thin thread has a light covering of wax. Before you thread beads on to it, dab the end with white glue to stop it fraying.

BRACELET/NECKLACE WIRE
This wire comes in a range of thicknesses. Ask an adult to help you cut it.

CLEAR PLASTIC TUBING
Plastic tubing comes in a wide range of widths and can be bought from hardware stores and gardening suppliers.

CLIP-ON EARRING ATTACHMENTS
Earring attachments are made of metal and are glued on to the back of home-made earrings. They clip the earrings on to your ear lobes.

COTTON KNITTING YARN
Use cotton knitting yarn when you want to make a thick bracelet or anklet, as it is very chunky. It is available in many bright shades.

DOWEL ROD
A smooth round wooden stick that is available in various thicknesses. It can be purchased from hardware stores.

FABRIC
To make some of the projects you will need a piece of plain, lightweight fabric.

Fabric

Felt

Cardboard

White glue

FELT
This is a type of fabric that is easy to cut and will not fray. It comes in many shades. You can buy it in fabric and hobby stores.

HAIR CLIP
This hair accessory has a metal clip that grips the hair. The top of the hair clip is made of a piece of smooth plastic.

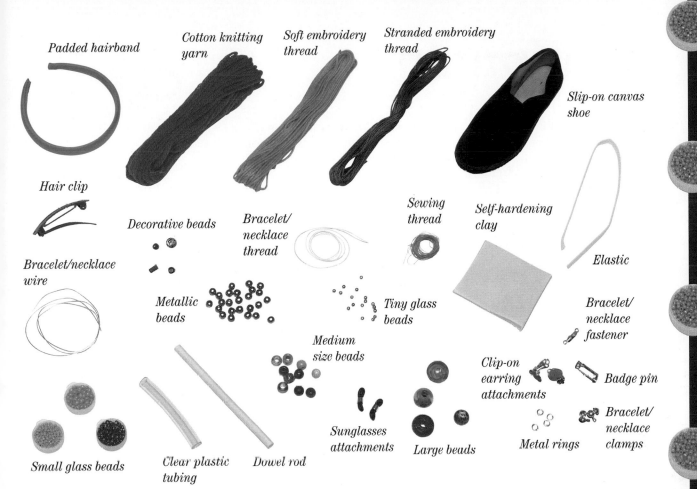

Padded hairband

Cotton knitting yarn

Soft embroidery thread

Stranded embroidery thread

Slip-on canvas shoe

Hair clip

Decorative beads

Bracelet/ necklace thread

Sewing thread

Self-hardening clay

Elastic

Bracelet/necklace wire

Metallic beads

Tiny glass beads

Bracelet/ necklace fastener

Medium size beads

Clip-on earring attachments

Badge pin

Sunglasses attachments

Large beads

Metal rings

Bracelet/ necklace clamps

Small glass beads

Clear plastic tubing

Dowel rod

METAL RINGS
Small loops used to attach bracelet or necklace fasteners.

PADDED HAIRBAND
This hairband is filled with soft padding and covered in fabric.

SELF-HARDENING CLAY
This material hardens in about 24 hours without baking.

SOFT EMBROIDERY THREAD
Soft embroidery thread is a thick thread that is ideal for making friendship bracelets.

STRANDED EMBROIDERY THREAD
This is a cotton thread made up of many strands. It is very good for making patterned and knotted friendship bracelets.

SUNGLASSES ATTACHMENTS
These rubber loops are used to attach sunglasses to a strap. You can buy them from specialist bead stores.

WHITE GLUE
Also known as PVA glue, this is a strong adhesive that will stick paper, fabrics and plastic.

Equipment

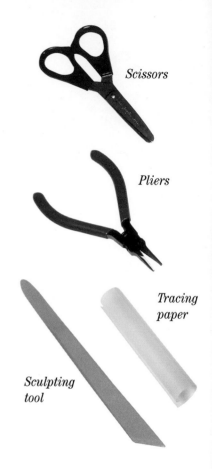

Scissors

Pliers

Tracing paper

Sculpting tool

BEADING NEEDLE
A beading needle is a very thin and pliable needle. It is used for sewing small beads on to fabric. As the needle is so fine, it should not be used for sewing through tough fabric.

ELECTRICAL TAPE
This is a type of strong adhesive tape. It is very good for fastening threads to a work surface. You can buy it from electrical and hardware stores.

FRETSAW
A fretsaw is a fine saw used for cutting through small pieces of wood. Always ask an adult to help you use a fretsaw properly.

PAINTBRUSH
Small and medium size paintbrushes are recommended for the projects in this book. Use them to dab on spots of white glue or to apply varnish, as well as for painting. Wash your paintbrushes after use to keep them in good condition.

PAPER
You will need a piece of paper to make a funnel. The funnel will help you to pour small beads into a tube or back into a container. You may also like to design some of your projects on paper before you start working on them.

PENCIL
Use a dark pencil to trace templates on to tracing paper. It is better if the pencil is not too sharp. Do not press too hard when you trace, or the pencil will tear the paper and you will have to start again.

PINS
These are very sharp, so be careful when you handle them. Use pins to hold pieces of fabric together while you are sewing. Remove the pins as you sew.

PLIERS
Use small or snub-nosed pliers to bend and cut bracelet or necklace wire, to open and close metal rings and to secure bracelet or necklace clamps. Many types of pliers have a cutting edge, so always ask for adult help when you use pliers.

ROLLING PIN
You will need a rolling pin to flatten and smooth clay. This is best done on a chopping board. Remember to wash the rolling pin thoroughly after use.

RULER
Use to measure lengths of thread and to draw straight lines.

SAFETY PINS
Safety pins have all sorts of uses. In this book, a safety pin is used to help thread elastic through a tube of fabric and to make a hair scrunchy.

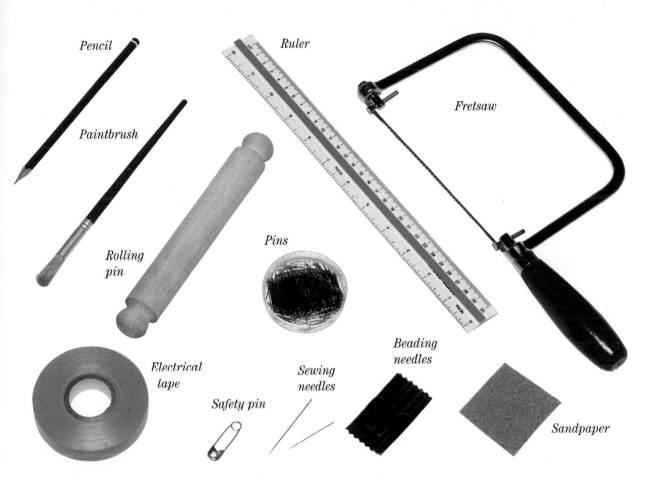

Pencil

Ruler

Paintbrush

Fretsaw

Rolling pin

Pins

Beading needles

Electrical tape

Sewing needles

Safety pin

Sandpaper

SANDPAPER
Used for smoothing wood that has rough edges, sandpaper is sometimes called glasspaper.

SCISSORS
Scissors are often very sharp, so be very careful when using them. It is a good idea to have two pairs of scissors, one pair for cutting fabric and the other pair for cutting paper.

SCULPTING TOOL
This is used for cutting and decorating clay before it hardens. Always clean the tool after use.

SEWING NEEDLE
Needles come in a wide range of sizes. Standard size needles are good for general sewing and for attaching medium size beads. You will need a large, strong

needle for sewing large beads on to coarse or thick fabric.

TRACING PAPER
This is special paper that can be seen through. You can buy pads of tracing paper in stationery stores or art stores. Baking parchment can be used instead, if you have trouble finding it. Do not press too hard when tracing, or you might tear the paper.

Basic Techniques

STARTING OFF

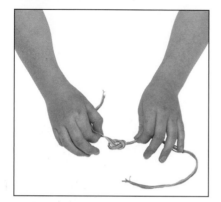

1 Cut the threads to the length asked for and tie together in a knot about 10cm/4in from the end.

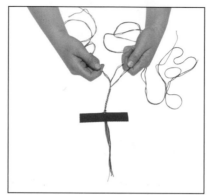

2 Tape the threads to your work surface using electrical tape just above the knot. Then work a 5cm/2in braid if asked for in the text.

3 Secure the end of the braided section to the work surface with electrical tape. Press the tape firmly over the threads.

FINISHING OFF

To finish a bracelet – divide the threads into three even groups and braid together. Tie a knot at the end of the braid and trim the threads.

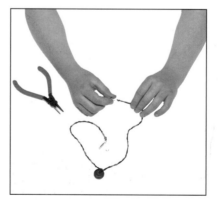

To finish a necklace – close a necklace clamp over each knot. Attach a metal ring to each clamp and fix a fastener on to the rings.

To finish a headband – tie a knot close to the end and thread on beads at each end. To hold the beads in place, tie another knot.

TYING ON

Tying on a bracelet – ask a friend to help tie the knot. If there is no one around to help, you could tie it around your ankle instead.

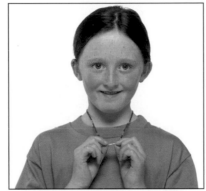

Fastening a necklace – place the necklace around your neck with the opened fasteners at the front. To line up the clasps, look in a mirror.

Tying on a headband – if you cannot do it yourself, ask a friend to tie the ends in a knot or in a bow at the back of your head.

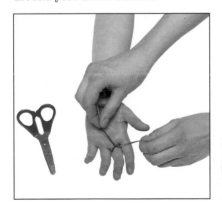

Tying on a ring – ask a friend to tie the ends in a double knot so that the ring will not come undone. Your friend can then carefully trim the remaining threads for you.

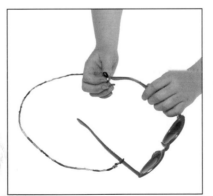

Attaching a sunglasses strap – finish as for a necklace, but attach a rubber loop to each ring. Then thread a loop on to each arm of the sunglasses.

Decorating clothing – use chalk to draw a shape on to the material. Lay a bracelet on top. Sew it on using a thread that matches the design of the bracelet.

11

Tracing a Template

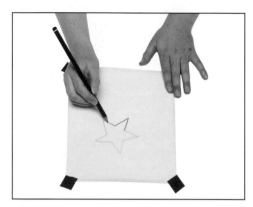

1 Place a piece of tracing paper over the template and secure it at the corners with tape. Carefully draw around the shape using a soft pencil.

2 Take the tracing paper off the template and turn the paper over. Rub over the traced image with the pencil on the reverse side of the tracing paper.

3 Place the tracing paper on a piece of stiff cardboard, with the traced outline face up. Draw firmly over the outline to transfer the template on to the cardboard.

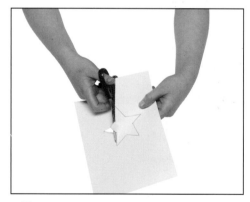

4 Cut out your template. To use a template on fabric, simply draw around the shape. Use a sculpting tool to outline the shape on to clay.

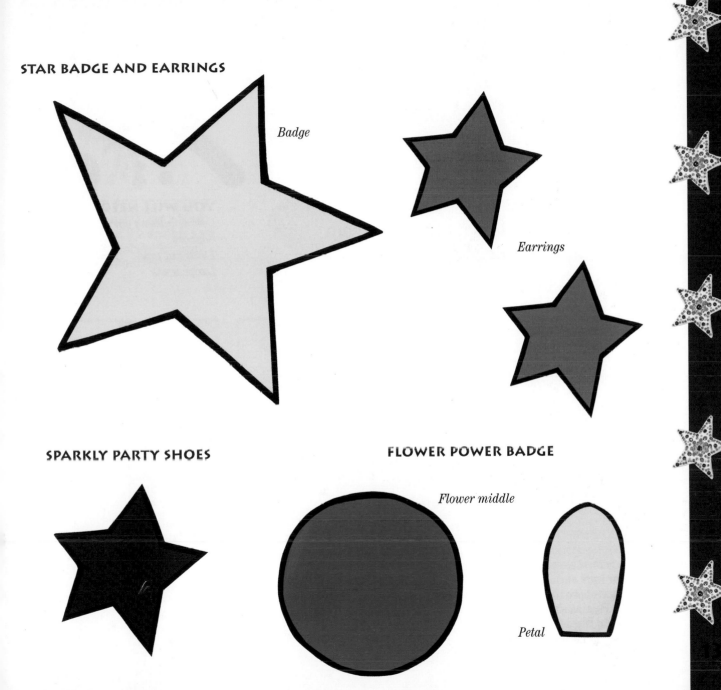

STAR BADGE AND EARRINGS

Badge

Earrings

SPARKLY PARTY SHOES

FLOWER POWER BADGE

Flower middle

Petal

Three Threads Bracelet

This bracelet is very simple to make because it uses only three threads of chunky cotton knitting yarn. If you are new to braiding, this is a good bracelet to start with. Make two matching bracelets so that you can wear one on your wrist and the other on your ankle.

YOU WILL NEED
Cotton knitting yarn
Scissors
Electrical tape
Large beads

1 Cut one piece of thread 130cm/4½ft long and two pieces 40cm/16in long. Tie the threads together in a knot 10cm/4in from the top and fasten them to your work surface with a piece of tape just above the knot. Lay the threads out as shown, with the long dark blue thread on the far right.

2 Weave the dark blue thread over the pale blue thread and under the yellow thread, then over the yellow thread and under the pale blue thread, as shown.

3 Hold the pale blue and yellow threads. Pull the dark blue thread gently, so that the loop you have made slides tightly up to the knot at the top. Continue repeating steps 2 and 3 until the bracelet is long enough to fit around your wrist or ankle.

4 Tie a knot and thread a bead on to the end. Tie another knot to hold the bead in place. Trim any uneven threads with scissors.

HANDY HINT
Make sure you hold the threads tight and straight while you are weaving, or the bracelet will curl up and become crooked.

Woven Bracelet

To make this very popular style of friendship bracelet you use a weaving technique that is easy to learn. If you want to make a really wide bracelet, weave two or three bracelets and then sew them together using stranded embroidery thread and a large sewing needle.

YOU WILL NEED
Cotton knitting yarn
Scissors
Electrical tape

1 Cut two threads in one shade and two in another, each 80cm/32in long. Fold them in half and tie the ends by the fold in a knot, 5cm/2in from the top. Fasten the threads to your work surface with tape close to the knot. Arrange the threads in pairs as shown.

2 Start with the far right pair of threads (in this project they are blue) and take them under the blue pair and purple pair next to them, then back over the purple pair. Leave them in the middle.

3 Take the pair of purple threads on the far left which you have not used yet. Take these threads under the purple and blue pairs next to them, then back over the blue pair. Leave the purple pair in the middle.

Hold the threads tightly when you are weaving, otherwise the threads will unwind and you will have to start all over again!

4 Pull the pairs of threads up tightly to the top. Then go back to the blue pair of threads on the far right and repeat steps 2 and 3 until the bracelet is long enough to fit around your wrist or ankle.

5 Tie the threads in a knot at the end of the weaving. Snip the looped threads at the top of the braid. You can leave the ends as they are or braid them.

17

Stripes Galore Bracelet

This is one of the most popular styles of friendship bracelet and, if you are a beginner, it is a good one to start with. The more threads you have, the wider the bracelet will be. The more different shades you use, the brighter it will be.

YOU WILL NEED
Stranded embroidery thread
Scissors
Electrical tape

1 You will need six threads, 100cm/40in long, two of each shade. Tie them together in a knot, 10cm/4in from the top of the threads. Tape the threads on to your work surface, close to the knot. Lay the threads out as shown.

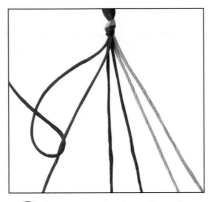

2 Start with the thread on the far left (in this project it is a pink thread). Take the thread over the pink thread next to it, then back under the thread, through the loop and over itself. Pull the thread gently to make a knot.

3 Repeat step 2. Still using the same thread, make two knots on the purple thread. Continue to knot the remaining purple and green threads with the pink thread in the same way until you reach the end of the first row.

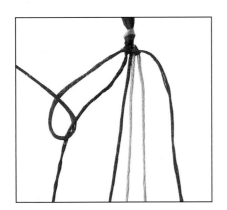

4 Go back to the new thread on the far left, which is another pink thread, and repeat steps 2 and 3 to make another row. Now the new thread on the far left will be a purple thread. Knot this in the same way.

5 Continue knotting each new far left thread over the other threads to build up stripes of the three different shades. Keep going until the bracelet is the right length to fit around your wrist or ankle.

6 Tie the threads at the end of the braid in a knot. Braid the loose threads at both ends of the bracelet for 6cm/2½in and secure with knots. Carefully trim any uneven threads with scissors.

Knotted Bracelet

The Knotted Bracelet uses a very simple knotting technique. If you make three bracelets the same length, why not twist them together to make a thicker bracelet?

YOU WILL NEED
Stranded embroidery thread
Scissors
Electrical tape

1 You will need four threads, each 100cm/40in long. Tie them in a knot, 10cm/4in from the top. Tape the threads on to your work surface just above the knot. Lay out the threads as shown.

2 Take the thread on its own (in this project it is orange) and put it over the other threads, then under them and through the loop. Pull the thread up tightly, holding the other threads tightly as well.

3 Continue knotting the orange thread over the others in the same way until you have braided as much as you want of this shade. You can make the bands all the same size or vary them.

4 Take a new shade of thread (in this project it is dark pink) to make a new row of knots and place the orange thread with the other threads. Change threads again when you want a new shade.

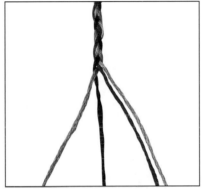

5 When the bracelet is long enough to fit around your wrist or ankle, tie the end of the braid in a knot to secure it.

6 Braid the loose threads at both ends for about 6cm/2½in and tie the ends in a knot. Trim any uneven threads with scissors.

Jungle Bracelet

This bracelet is inspired by the hues you would see on safari. You could choose your own theme, such as a rainbow, a sunset or a season, and select shades to co-ordinate with that theme.

1 Cut five threads, three of one shade and two of another, each 100cm/40in long. Tie the threads in a knot, 15cm/6in from the top. Fasten the threads on to your work surface with tape just above the knot. Lay out the threads as shown.

YOU WILL NEED
Soft embroidery thread
Scissors
Electrical tape
Decorative beads

22

2 Start with the thread on the far left (in this project it is a brown thread). Take the thread over the orange thread on the right, then back under the thread, through the loop and over itself. Pull the thread gently to make a knot and repeat.

3 Continue the same knotting technique as in step 2, making two knots on each of the remaining threads on the right, until you get to the end of the first row.

4 Take the new thread on the far left (an orange thread) and make a new row of knots as shown in steps 2 and 3.

5 Continue knotting the bracelet until it is the right length to fit around your wrist or ankle. Tie the threads in a knot to secure the end of the knotted braid.

6 Braid the loose threads for 4cm/1⅛in and tie the end of the braid in a knot. Thread a bead on to each loose thread and tie a knot behind the bead to stop it from falling off.

23

Hair Wrap

These braids look great! Take it in turns with a friend to do each other's hair. Finish off the braid with two beads tied on to the end.

YOU WILL NEED
Stranded embroidery thread
Scissors
Medium size beads

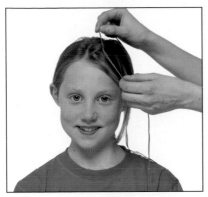

1 Cut two lengths of different shades of thread, twice the length of the hair you are braiding. Fold the threads in half to find the middle. Take a 1cm/½in section of hair and knot the middle of the threads around it, close to the scalp.

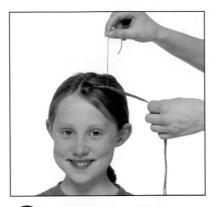

2 Hold the section of hair away from the head. Select one shade of thread and start winding it tightly around the hair and the other threads.

3 When you have wound as much as you want of the first shade, swap the thread for another and continue winding in the same way. Keep alternating until you reach the end of the hair.

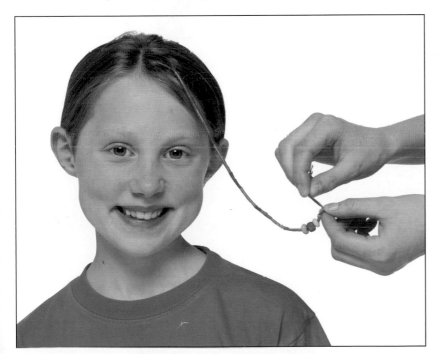

4 To finish off, thread a few beads on to the end of the hair and tie a knot in the thread to stop the beads falling off. Knot the threads around the hair to stop the wrap from coming undone. When you want to remove the wrap, cut off the knot and beads at the end of the wrap and unwind the threads.

Twisty Bracelet

This bracelet is almost like mixing a palette of different paints, but instead of using paints you are twisting threads together to make new shades.

YOU WILL NEED
Stranded embroidery thread
Scissors
Electrical tape

HANDY HINT
Be sure to hold on tightly to the twisted braid. If you let go before you have secured it with a knot, the twist will unwind.

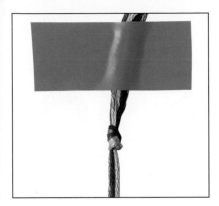

1 You will need six threads, each 70cm/28in long. Tie them in a knot, 10cm/4in from the top of the threads. Fasten them on to your work surface with tape just above the knot.

2 Hold the ends of the threads together and twist them together in the same direction until they feel tight. The threads will start to get shorter.

3 Pull the twisted length straight and place your finger in the middle of it. Fold the twisted length in half, then remove your finger and watch the threads twist together.

4 Remove the tape and knot the free ends together. Trim any uneven threads with scissors. To fasten the bracelet around your wrist, push the knot at one end through the loop at the other.

Beady Bangle

For this project you will need a piece of clear plastic tubing. It can be bought from most do-it-yourself stores or gardening suppliers. Plastic tubing comes in a range of sizes, so you could make lots of different sized bracelets.

YOU WILL NEED

Sewing thread
Scissors
Clear plastic tubing
Dowel rod (to fit the width of the plastic tubing)

Fretsaw
Sandpaper
Paper
Small beads
Electrical tape

1 Tie a strand of thread around your wrist. This bracelet must be large enough to be removed by pulling your hand through it. When you have found the right size, cut the bracelet and lay it next to the plastic tubing. Cut the tubing to the same length.

2 Ask an adult to cut a 2cm/⅝in piece of dowel rod with a fretsaw, then smooth the ends of the dowel rod with a piece of sandpaper. Firmly push half the dowel rod into one end of the plastic tubing.

3 Roll a piece of paper into a cone-shaped funnel that will fit into the end of the tube. Pour the beads into the cone and fill up the tube. Leave 1cm/½in at the end of the tube empty. If you want a striped bracelet, pour in different shade beads in separate layers.

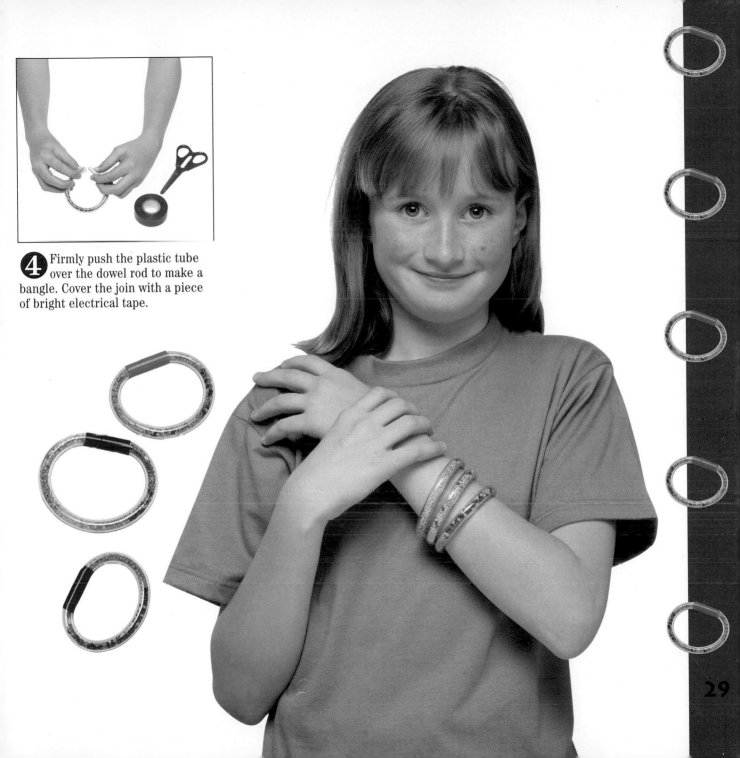

4 Firmly push the plastic tube over the dowel rod to make a bangle. Cover the join with a piece of bright electrical tape.

29

Sunglasses Strap

A strap is very useful and great fun to wear. When you do not want to wear your sunnies, you can hang them around your neck.

YOU WILL NEED

Stranded embroidery thread
Scissors
Electrical tape
2 necklace clamps and metal rings
Pliers
2 rubber sunglasses attachments

1 You will need six strands of thread, each 200cm/6½ft long. Tie the threads together in a knot, 5cm/2in from the top of the threads. Tape them on to your work surface just above the knot. Lay the threads out as shown.

2 Take the single thread that is out on its own (in this project it is dark red) and put it over the other threads, then under them and through the loop. Pull the thread up tightly, holding the other threads tightly as well.

3 Continue knotting this single thread over the others until you have as much as you want of that shade and want to change it.

4 Take a new shade of thread and place the dark red thread with the others. Make a row of knots as explained in step 2. Continue knotting in this way and changing the shade as often as you wish.

5 When the knotted cord is about 70cm/28in long, tie the threads in a tight knot close to the braid. Now you will need to trim the loose threads very close to the knot at each end. Be careful not to cut the knots themselves.

6 Attach a clamp over each knot and close the clamps. Attach a metal ring to each clamp and a rubber loop to each ring. Thread the rubber loops over the arms of your sunglasses and tighten the loops around the arms.

HANDY HINT

A pair of pliers and some adult help will make it easy to attach and close the clamps and metal rings.

Stripes and Beads

This bracelet has beads threaded into it to add extra brightness, sparkle and texture. Use small or medium size beads, but make sure the hole of each bead is large enough for the thread to fit through.

YOU WILL NEED
Soft embroidery thread
Scissors
Electrical tape
Small and medium beads

1 You will need four threads, each 100cm/40in long. Tie the threads in a knot, 10cm/4in from the top of the threads. Fasten them to your work surface with tape just above the knot and lay them out as shown.

2 Start with the thread on the far left (in this project it is purple). Take the thread over the pink thread next to it and back under, through the loop and over itself. Pull the thread gently to make a knot and repeat the knot again.

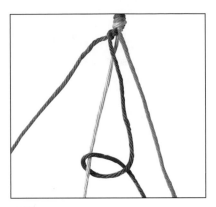

3 Do the same knots on the blue and the orange threads. You will now have finished the first row and the purple thread should be on the right.

4 Go back to the new thread on the far left (a pink thread) and, before you start making a new row of knots, thread a bead on to it. When the bead has been threaded on, continue to knot over the other threads to finish the row.

5 Go back to the new thread on the far left (pale blue). Knot the thread over the first two threads (orange and purple) and, before you knot it over the pink, thread a bead on to the pink thread and then knot the pale blue thread over it.

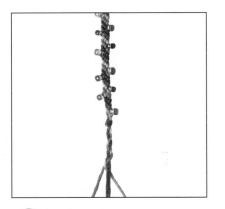

6 Continue to knot and thread on beads until the bracelet is the right length. Tie the threads in a knot. Braid the loose threads at both ends for about 6cm/2½in before tying knots. Thread a bead on to the end of each braid and secure with a knot.

Beaded Hair Clip

This hair clip really stands out when it is in the hair. It looks great with any hairstyle.

YOU WILL NEED
Soft embroidery thread
Scissors
Electrical tape
Small and medium beads
Plain hair clip
White glue

1 You will need ten lengths of thread, two of each shade and each 80cm/32in long. Tie the threads in a knot, 15cm/6in from the top. Fasten the threads to your work surface with tape just above the knot. Lay the threads out in pairs as shown.

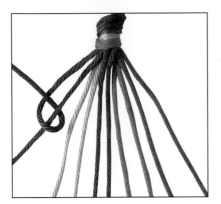

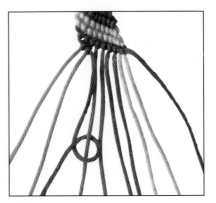

2 Start with the thread on the far left (in this project it is a dark blue thread). Take the thread over the dark blue thread next to it, back under the thread, through the loop and over itself. Pull the thread gently and repeat the knot again.

3 Do the same knots on the other threads in the row until the thread you started with is at the end of the row. Go back to the new thread on the far left (another dark blue thread) and repeat the knots explained in steps 2 and 3.

4 Continue knotting the rows with each new far left thread, building up stripes of different shades, until the braid is long enough to fit on the hair clip.

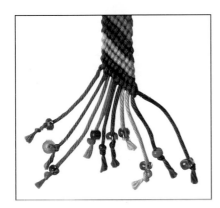

5 Thread small beads on to the end of each thread and tie the end of each thread in a firm knot to stop the beads falling off.

6 Apply white glue sparingly on to the back of the braid. Open out the clip and stick the braid on to the back. Fold the knotted end of the braid to the underside of the clip and glue. When dry, trim any excess threads.

HANDY HINT
To put dangling beads on to the other end of your braid, carefully undo the knot and follow the instructions in step 5 before sticking the braid to the clip.

Star Badge & Earrings

This glitzy badge gleams with shiny beads. Why not make a pair of earrings to match it? The earrings are just as easy to make as the badge, but do not forget to make two!

YOU WILL NEED
Pencil
Tracing paper
Cardboard
Rolling pin
Self-hardening clay
Sculpting tool
Beads
Paintbrush
White glue
Felt
Badge pin
Clip-on earring
  attachments

1 Make the star templates as shown on pages 12–13. With a rolling pin, roll out a piece of clay 5mm/¼in thick. Place the templates on the clay and cut around them with a sculpting tool.

2 Position the beads on the clay stars in your chosen pattern and then, very gently press the beads a little into the clay. This will stop the beads from coming loose.

3 Paint a coat of glue over the beaded stars. This will help seal the beads in the clay and give the stars a smooth finish. Leave the stars in a warm place to dry. The clay will harden in about 24 hours.

4 Place the templates on a piece of felt, draw around them and cut out. Glue the felt stars to the back of the badge and earrings. Glue the badge pin and clip-on earring attachments to the felt. Allow to dry before wearing your new accessories.

Knotty Dotty Necklace

Choose lots of the beads that you like best to knot into this bright necklace, or select one really beautiful big bead to knot halfway along the necklace. If you do not have a fastener to secure your necklace around your neck, tie the ends in a knot.

YOU WILL NEED
Stranded embroidery thread
Scissors
Electrical tape
Small and medium beads

2 necklace clamps
2 metal rings
Necklace fastener
Pliers

1 You will need four threads, two of each shade and each 150cm/5ft long. Tie the threads together in a knot, 10cm/4in from the top. Fasten them to your work surface with tape just above the knot. Lay the threads out as shown.

2 Start with the thread that is out on its own (in this project it is blue). Take it over the other threads, then under them and through the loop. Pull the thread up tightly, holding the other threads tightly at the same time.

3 After you have knotted a row of about five knots, thread a bead on to the blue thread and then continue to make a few more knots.

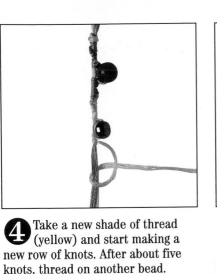

4 Take a new shade of thread (yellow) and start making a new row of knots. After about five knots, thread on another bead. Continue making rows of knots and adding beads in this way.

5 When the necklace is the length you want, tie all the threads together in a knot.

6 Trim the threads close to the knot at each end. Attach a necklace clamp over each knot and a metal ring to each clamp. Then attach half the necklace fastener to each of the metal rings.

Rainbow Necklace

This necklace is simply stunning. Not only is it a great piece to add to your own jewel box, but it would make a very special present for a friend. You will need a lot of beads to make the Rainbow Necklace.

YOU WILL NEED
Necklace thread
Scissors
White glue
Necklace fastener
Small and medium beads

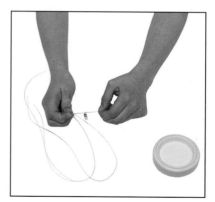

1 You will need three different lengths of necklace thread, one 50cm/20in long, one 60cm/24in long and one 70cm/28in long. Dab the thread ends with glue to stop fraying, then group the threads together and knot them on to one end of the necklace fastener.

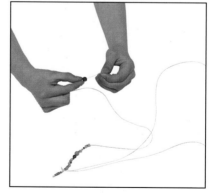

2 Decide which shade(s) you are going to use for each strand, and work out a pattern using all the different sizes of beads. Start with your first group of beads and thread them on to one of the strands, leaving 10cm/4in of necklace thread spare at the end.

3 Move on to the next strand and thread on a new shade of beads. Do the same for the third strand. Do not forget to leave 10cm/4in of thread spare at the end of each beaded strand.

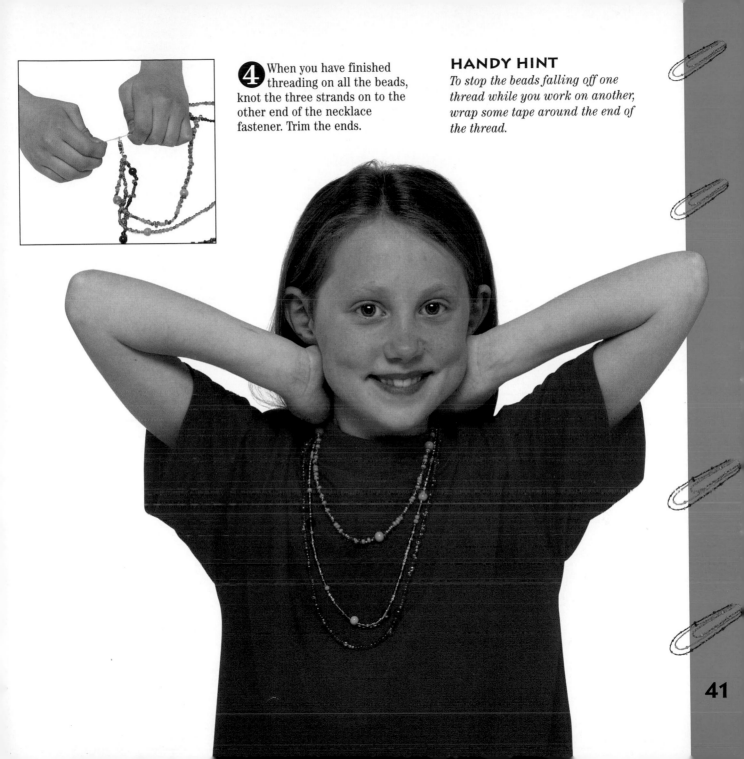

4 When you have finished threading on all the beads, knot the three strands on to the other end of the necklace fastener. Trim the ends.

HANDY HINT

To stop the beads falling off one thread while you work on another, wrap some tape around the end of the thread.

41

Glitzy Hairband

Create your own designer hairband by simply sewing an assortment of beads on to a padded hairband.

YOU WILL NEED
Felt
Scissors
White glue
Paintbrush
Padded hairband
Tiny and small beads
Beading needle
Sewing thread

42

1 Cut out small dots of felt in lots of different shades. The dots can be the same shade as the beads, or in contrasting ones.

2 Dab a small spot of glue on to the padded hairband where you want each dot to be. Stick the felt dots on and let the glue dry.

3 When the glue is completely dry, carefully sew a bead on to the middle of each felt dot. To make sure that the beads do not come loose, do two stitches for each bead. Then knot the thread around the bead. Cut the thread as close as possible to the knot. Do the same for all the remaining beads.

4 To make a different style of hairband, select a mixture of beads in shades that co-ordinate with the hairband, or create a rainbow effect by sewing your beads in rows of a single shade.

Spiral Bracelet & Ring

This bracelet is made from wire, so it can be coiled and worn anywhere on your arm or even on your leg! The ring is simply a beaded loop of wire.

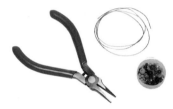

YOU WILL NEED
Pliers
Bracelet wire
Small and medium beads

SAFETY NOTE
You will need an adult to help you cut and twist the wire for this project.

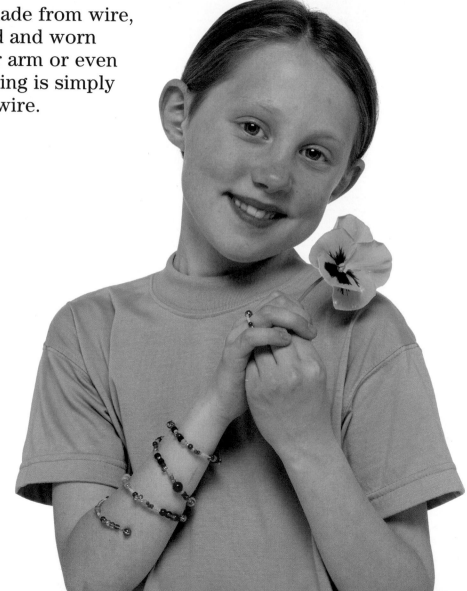

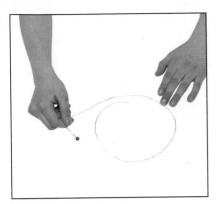

1 Cut a piece of brass wire 60cm/24in long using a pair of pliers. Thread a medium size bead on to one end of the wire and secure it in place by bending and twisting the wire with the pliers.

2 Thread a bright assortment of beads on to the wire, leaving 5cm/2in of wire at the end free.

3 Thread another medium size bead on to the end. Bend and twist the wire to secure it in place. Trim the ends and coil the bracelet around your arm in a spiral.

4 To make a ring, cut a length of wire three times the width of your finger. Bend it in a U-shape and thread on enough beads so that the ring fits comfortably. Twist the two ends of wire together and then press them flat. Snip off excess wire with a pair of pliers.

Funky Chunky Bracelet

This chunky bracelet uses ten strands of knitting yarn. You have to hold the threads firmly, or the weaving will be uneven.

YOU WILL NEED
Cotton knitting yarn
Scissors
Electrical tape

1 You will need five different shades of thread, each 80cm/32in long. Fold the threads in half and tie in a knot, 5cm/2in from the fold. Tape the threads to your work surface just above the knot. Lay the threads out as shown.

2 Start with the far right pair of threads (in this project they are yellow) and weave them over the pink pair, under the pale blue pair, over the green pair and under the purple pair. Pull the yellow pair up tightly and leave on the left.

3 Take the pink pair on the far right and weave them over the pale blue pair, under the green pair, over the purple pair and under the yellow pair. Pull the threads up tightly and leave on the left.

4 Keep weaving in the same way, with each new pair of threads on the far right as shown in steps 2 and 3, until you have a braid long enough to fit around your wrist or ankle. Tie the end in a knot and cut the top loop. Trim any uneven threads with scissors.

47

Hippy Headband

Dress up as a happy hippy and wear this bright band around your head. The more threads you use, the wider the braid will be.

YOU WILL NEED
Stranded embroidery thread
Scissors
Electrical tape
Large beads

HANDY HINT
To make it easy to thread the beads on to your headband, wrap a little tape around the end of the threads. This will keep the threads together and stop them fraying.

48

1 Cut 12 lengths of thread, each 150cm/5ft long. Tie them in a knot 15cm/6in from the top of the threads and fasten them on to your work surface with a piece of tape just above the knot.

2 Divide the threads into three groups, each with four threads. Continue braiding the threads until the band is long enough to fit around your head.

3 Tie the threads at the end of the braid in a firm knot.

4 Thread beads on to both ends and secure them with knots. Thread another bead to each end and tie another knot. Trim any uneven threads. To make a bracelet, cut 12 threads, each 40cm/16in.

49

Arrow Bracelet

You can make the Arrow Bracelet using two, three or four different shades of thread. If you want a thicker bracelet, use more threads.

YOU WILL NEED
Soft embroidery thread
Scissors
Electrical tape

1 You will need eight pieces of thread, four of each shade and each 100cm/40in long. Tie them in a knot 5cm/2in from the top and then braid them together for 5cm/2in. Tape the threads to your work surface and lay them out as shown.

2 Start with the thread on the far left (in this project it is an orange thread) and do two knots on each of the three threads next to it on the right. Leave the thread in the middle.

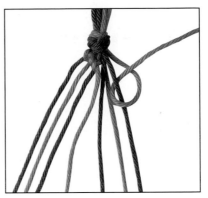

3 Now take the orange thread on the far right and do two knots on each of the three threads next to it on the left. Leave the orange thread in the middle.

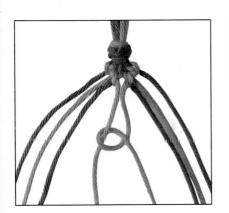

4 Take the middle right orange thread and make two knots over the orange thread on the left.

5 Repeat steps 2, 3 and 4 until the bracelet is long enough to fit around your wrist or ankle.

6 Braid the threads for 5cm/2in and secure with a knot. Trim any uneven threads with scissors.

Flower Power Badge

This jazzy little Flower Power Badge is sure to add a splash of brightness to a plain T-shirt, jumper, hat or backpack. Do not be surprised when all your friends want one too!

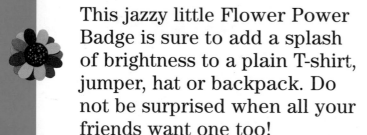

YOU WILL NEED
Pencil
Tracing paper
Cardboard
Felt
Scissors
Sewing thread
Sewing needle
Tiny and small beads
White glue
Badge pin

1 Make the templates for the petals and flower middle as shown on pages 12–13. Draw around the templates on different shades of felt. You will need two middle circles and 16 petals. Cut out.

2 Sew the beads on to one of the felt circles. You can use lots of beads so the felt is totally covered, or just dot the beads about to make a simple pattern.

3 Turn the beaded circle over and glue the petals all around the edge, mixing the shades as you go. Apply more glue and stick on the second layer of petals.

4 On the other circle of felt, glue or sew on the badge pin and then stick this circle on to the back of the flower. Leave the glue to dry before trying on the badge.

Scrummy Scrunchy

This beautiful hair accessory will make your pony tail very eye-catching. Why not design it to match your best outfit or hairband? For a special occasion, make a Scrummy Scrunchy from black velvet fabric and shiny metallic beads in gold or silver.

YOU WILL NEED

Fabric
Scissors
Tiny and small beads
Beading needle

Sewing thread
Sewing needle
1cm/½in wide elastic
Safety pin

1 Cut a piece of fabric, 30cm/1ft x 12cm/5in. Fold each long side of the fabric over to the wrong side by 1cm/½in and ask an adult to iron them flat. Sew beads on to the right side of the fabric, 2cm/1in in from the edges.

2 Fold the fabric (beads on the inside) in half lengthways and stitch the two short edges together. Leave a 1cm/½in gap in the middle.

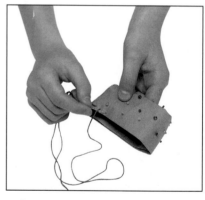

3 Turn the fabric right side out. The beads will be on the outside. Fold the fabric widthways so that the two seams join each other. Sew around the edge with thread in a matching shade.

4 Cut a length of elastic 40cm/ 16in long and fasten a safety pin to one end. Thread the pin and elastic through the gap and feed it all the way around until it comes back to the gap.

5 Pull the pin out of the gap and unclip it from the elastic. Pull the elastic gently to make the fabric ruffle. Tie the elastic in a knot or sew the elastic together to secure it. Trim any excess elastic.

6 Sew up the gap with a small slip stitch. It is important, especially for this step, that the sewing thread is the same shade as the fabric.

HANDY HINT

To stop the beads coming loose, use a double thickness of sewing thread and sew each bead twice. Tie a knot when you have finished sewing.

55

Square Deal

This is one of the more complicated bracelets. If you are not pleased with your first attempt, keep on trying until you become an expert.

YOU WILL NEED
Soft embroidery thread
Scissors
Electrical tape

1 Cut two threads of one shade and four of another, each 100cm/40in long. Tie the threads in a knot and braid them together for 5cm/2in. Fasten the threads on to your work surface with tape above the knot and at the end of the braid.

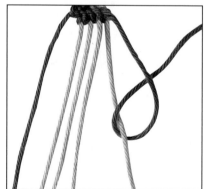

2 When you have laid your threads out, as shown in step 1, you are ready to start the Square Deal. Knot the thread on the far left (in this project it is dark blue) over the threads to the right. Do two knots on each thread.

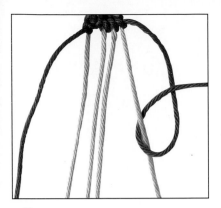

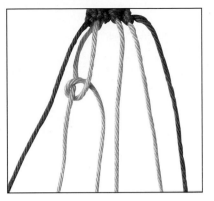

3 Knot the new far left thread, which is dark blue, over the pale blue thread next to it and do two knots. Knot the far right thread over the pale blue thread to the left and do two knots.

4 Take the pale blue thread that is second on the left and knot it over the next pale blue thread. Do two knots. Then knot it over the other pale blue threads on the right. Do only one knot on each.

5 Repeat step 3 and then repeat step 4 until you have woven four rows of pale blue threads between outside edges of dark blue. Make sure you braid the correct thread each time.

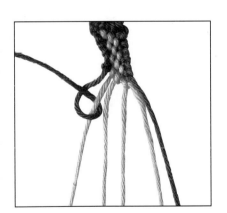

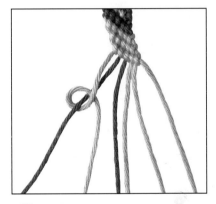

6 Take the dark blue thread on the left and make a knot on the pale blue thread next to it. Do two knots and return the thread to the starting position. Do the same with the dark blue thread on the far right.

7 Knot the far left dark blue thread over all the threads on the right until the end of the row to complete the square. Now knot the far left pale blue thread over all the threads on the right until you get to the end of the row.

8 Continue knotting the far left thread over the other threads until there is a dark blue thread on either side of the pale blue threads. You are now ready to go back to step 2. When the bracelet is the right length, braid 5cm/2in and tie a knot.

Os and Xs

The Os and Xs bracelet will really impress your friends! It looks terrific in black and white, but it could also be braided to match the strip of the football team you follow.

YOU WILL NEED
Soft embroidery thread
Scissors
Electrical tape

1 You will need eight pieces of thread, four of each shade and each 100cm/40in long. Tie the threads together in a knot and braid them for 5cm/2in. Tape the threads to your work surface at the end of the braid and lay them out as shown.

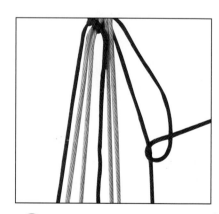

2 Take the thread on the far left (in this project it is purple) and tie two knots on each of the three threads to its right. Leave the thread in the middle. Repeat with the purple thread on the far right.

3 Take the purple thread on the middle right and knot it over the middle left thread. Do two knots. Repeat steps 2 and 3 using the three outer pairs of threads. Start with the outermost thread on the left.

4 Your bracelet now has four rows of braiding, two rows in each shade. Now knot the far right purple thread over the purple thread next to it. Do two knots. Now repeat, using the far left purple thread.

5 Using the fourth thread from the left, do three knots on each of the three threads to its left. Repeat, using the fourth thread from the right.

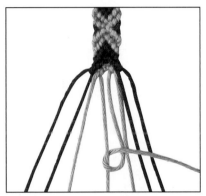

6 Knot the new middle right thread over the middle left thread. Do two knots and then repeat all of step 5. You have made an 'X'. Repeat steps 5 and 6 using the two pairs of purple threads.

7 Knot the middle left pink thread over the thread to its left. Do two knots. Repeat, using the middle right pink thread. Next, knot the middle right thread over the middle left thread. Do two knots.

8 To complete the design, repeat from step 2 onwards until your bracelet is the right length. To finish the bracelet, braid 5cm/2in and tie a knot. Trim any uneven threads with scissors.

Sparkly Party Shoes

These beaded shoes are great fun to wear at a party and will make your party outfit look extra special.

YOU WILL NEED

Plain slip-on canvas shoes
Strong sewing needle
Sewing thread
Small and medium beads
Pencil
Tracing paper
Cardboard
Scissors
Felt
White glue
Paintbrush

1 Starting at the toe of one shoe, begin to sew on beads using sewing thread and needle. When the thread runs out, tie a knot, re-thread the needle and start again.

2 Cover as much of the shoe as possible with beads. Repeat step 1 for the other shoe. Each shoe can have different beads, so do not worry about matching them exactly.

3 Make the star template as shown on pages 12-13. Use the cut out template to draw two stars on a piece of felt. Cut out the stars and sew on some small beads.

4 Glue a star on to the elasticated panel of each shoe. Leave the glue to dry thoroughly before trying on your dazzling new dancing shoes.

Tassely Bag

Tassels are a fun way of decorating a piece of clothing or an accessory. They could even be made into earrings or a brooch.

YOU WILL NEED
Soft embroidery thread
Scissors
Large sewing needle

HANDY HINT
Add extra sparkle to your tassels by threading a bead on to the end of some or all of the threads. Secure the bead with a knot.

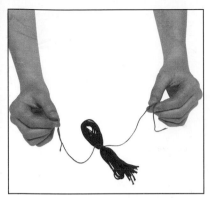

1 Cut six lengths of thread, each 60cm/24in long. Hold them together and fold them in half, then in half again. Knot a piece of thread, 30cm/12in long, around the middle of the bundle of yarns. Smooth the yarns to form the tassel.

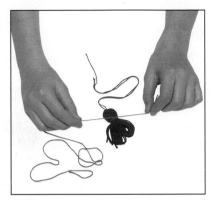

2 Cut a piece of thread 40cm/16in long and in a contrasting shade. Tie one end of it around the bundle, 2cm/1in from the top of the tassel. Make sure that one end of the thread is much longer than the other after the knot has been tied.

3 Thread the longer end through the needle. Working from left to right, pass the needle under the thread tied around the tassel then bring the needle back through the newly made loop. Do not pull tight. Repeat the stitch around the tassel.

4 When you have finished the first row, start to make the second row. Place the needle through a loop on the first row and bring it back through the newly made loop. Continue this stitch until you get to the top of the tassel.

5 Push the needle and thread up through the middle of the tassel. Knot the thread. Cut the looped threads at the end of the tassel. For a small tassel cut them short, or keep them long if you want to add beads to your tassel.

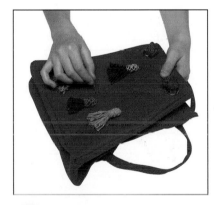

6 Use the threads at the top to sew the tassels on to a bag, or on to whatever you are decorating. Tassels look wonderful when they are used along with ribbon to decorate a present. They can also be used as Christmas tree decorations.

ACKNOWLEDGEMENTS

*The publishers would like to thank
the following children for appearing
in this book:*

Charlie Anderson

Kristina Chase

Vicky Dummigan

Sarah Kenna

Lee Knight

Mickey Melaku

Laura Masters

Fiona Mulcahy

Lucy Nightingale

Folake Ogundeyin

*Gratitude also to their parents and
Walnut Tree Walk Primary School.*

u